THE BRITISH MUSEUM

BRITAIN

THE BRITISH MUSEUM
BRITAIN

Lindsay Stainton

THE BRITISH MUSEUM PRESS

For HJFC

Endpapers: Hay-Makers (detail), 1791, stipple engraving
by George Stubbs (1724–1806)
Frontispiece: Durham Cathedral, 1806, watercolour over pencil
by John Sell Cotman (1782–1842)

Photography by British Museum Department of Photography
and Imaging (Saul Peckham)

© 2005 The Trustees of the British Museum
First published in 2005 by The British Museum Press
A division of The British Museum Company Ltd
38 Russell Square, London WC1B 3QQ

Lindsay Stainton has asserted her moral right to be identified
as the author of this work

A catalogue record for this book is available from the British Library

ISBN-13:   978-0-7141-5034-5
ISBN-10:   0 7141 5034 7

Designed and typeset in Centaur by Peter Ward
Printed in China by C&C Offset Printing Co.,Ltd.

CONTENTS

A SENSE OF PLACE

Conway Castle is among the most magnificent of Edward I's great Welsh fortresses, built between 1283 and 1289 as part of his campaign to secure the newly conquered principality. In 1346 major reconstruction work was carried out, and the rotting wooden trusses supporting the ceiling of the Great Hall were replaced with the stone arches seen here. From the late fifteenth century, with the Tudor accession to the English throne, the need for defensive strongholds in Wales disappeared and the castle fell into disrepair, unused for military purposes save for a brief episode during the Civil War of the 1640s. By the late eighteenth century, its ruined yet noble structure had become a picturesque attraction for travellers and artists.

Thomas Girtin made a sketching tour of North Wales in the summer of 1798, and of all the subjects he chose, this view of the Great Hall is among the most dramatic. The remains of the vaulting frame the image, and by viewing the building not from a distance but from the inside, he achieves an unusual sense of immediacy. He must also have had in mind his studies from the prints of Piranesi, with their evocation of ancient Rome's majestic ruins. The broad, loose application of paint and the schematic treatment of the foreground suggest that this sketch was probably drawn and coloured on the spot; it served as the model for a larger, more fully completed watercolour.

The Great Hall, Conway Castle, about 1798,
watercolour over pencil by Thomas Girtin (1775–1802)

THE MYSTERIOUS ancient monument of Stonehenge has inspired countless writers and artists. It is the memorable setting for the tragic climax of Thomas Hardy's 1891 novel *Tess of the D'Urbervilles*. Betrayed by the men she encounters and driven to murder a cruel lover, Tess finally takes refuge at Stonehenge with her husband Angel Clare in the 'black solitude' of night. Her experiences are intensified with descriptions of landscape: for her, Stonehenge represents both a joyful conclusion and an inevitable finality to their love. Anticipating her fate, Tess falls asleep on a great stone slab, almost as if she were a sacrificial offering – as dawn breaks the police arrive and she is arrested, sent for trial and hanged.

For Constable, Stonehenge represented his preoccupation with the passage of time. Here he contrasts the transience of a double rainbow with the monument's antiquity.

Stonehenge, 1836, watercolour with pencil and black chalk, squared for transfer by John Constable (1776–1837)

THE PALACE OF NONSUCH was begun by Henry VIII in 1538 as a celebration of his Tudor dynasty. Its remarkable stuccoed and gilded façade made it one of the most extraordinary buildings in sixteenth-century Europe. It was demolished in 1682.

APPELLATVM. NONCIVTZ
simile.

Nonsuch Palace, Surrey, 1568, pen and brown ink with brown wash
and watercolour by Joris Hoefnagel (1542–1600)

Overleaf: Windsor Castle, about 1829, watercolour
by Joseph Mallord William Turner (1775–1851)

London from the North, 1751,
pen and brown ink with grey wash over black chalk
by Giovanni Antonio Canaletto (1697–1768)

S T PAUL'S CATHEDRAL dominates this panoramic view of the city. Westminster Abbey is visible in the distance to the west, just beyond the newly completed Westminster Bridge, and dozens of parish church spires punctuate the skyline. Canaletto worked in England between 1746 and 1755.

WITH THE PUBLICATION of William Gilpin's *Observations on the River Wye . . .* in 1783, tourists began to visit the area in considerable numbers, many to admire the ruins at Tintern, 'which Nature has now made . . . her own'. Responding to the taste for antiquarian and picturesque subjects, the young Turner made annual sketching tours throughout Britain, visiting the Wye Valley in 1792 and 1793. His training as an architectural draughtsman enabled him to make the most of a subject such as this, but that was not the only reason he chose to concentrate on the soaring ivy-clad arches of the interior – Gilpin had also pointed out that the Abbey's exterior was disfigured by the shabby houses surrounding it, inhabited by importunate beggars, while within half a mile, great ironworks disturbed the tranquillity of the setting. Turner shows a group of visitors 'survey[ing] the whole in one view – the elements of air, and earth . . . and the grand and venerable remains', while they listen to a gardener who has set aside his wheelbarrow to act as their guide.

Wordsworth first visited the Wye, Gilpin in hand, in 1793, but his poem *Lines Written a Few Miles above Tintern Abbey* (1798) marks a new and more profound response to nature than hitherto attempted in poetry: memory and imagination are fused with an intensity of observation whose visual counterpart can be found in Turner's work of this same period.

Tintern Abbey, the Transept, about 1795, watercolour
by Joseph Mallord William Turner (1775–1851)

THE RUINS of Kirkstall, one of the great Cistercian abbeys founded in the twelfth century, survive in the outskirts of Leeds, but in 1800 this was still a secluded and rural valley. Girtin's Yorkshire subjects are among the most powerful he painted during his short career. Although this may seem a conventionally picturesque subject, he is more concerned with the transient effects of light and shade that animate the landscape, thereby achieving a monumentality that was entirely new in British painting.

Kirkstall Abbey, Yorkshire, 1800, watercolour over pencil by Thomas Girtin (1775–1802)

Rievaulx Abbey, Yorkshire,
1944, lithograph by
John Piper (1903–92)

Overleaf: Coventry,
Warwickshire, about 1832,
watercolour by Joseph
Mallord William Turner
(1775–1851)

AN ISLAND RACE

DESCRIBED by the medieval chron-
icler Matthew Paris as 'the very
front door of England', Dover was
historically also a bastion, with its
fortified castle and the cliffs forming a
natural line of defence. Shakespeare
Cliff is named for a scene — probably
written in Dover in 1604 — in *King Lear*
in which the Earl of Gloucester,
blinded for his loyalty to Lear, seeks
to end his life by throwing himself
from:

> . . . a cliff whose high and bending
>   head
> looks fearfully on the confined deep;
> Bring me to the very brim of it . . .
> . . . from that place
> I shall no leading need.

Shakespeare Cliff, Dover, about 1820,
watercolour by David Cox (1783–1859)

24

THIS PANORAMIC VIEW over a winding stretch of the Medway estuary, looking towards Sheerness in the distance, was drawn from the vantage point of Gillingham's church tower. It is unusually bold and atmospheric for its date.

Sheerness from the Tower of Gillingham Church, Kent, 1757,
watercolour over pencil by Jonathan Skelton (about 1735–59)

Overleaf: Dunstanborough Castle, Northumberland,
about 1840, watercolour with touches of bodycolour
by James Duffield Harding (1797–1863)

Bʀɪᴛᴀɪɴ's ᴄᴏᴀsᴛʟɪɴᴇ provided subjects for many nineteenth-century
artists, whether the stormy seas of J. D.
Harding's Dunstanborough Castle (see
previous pages) or this tranquil scene
of fishermen at work by Callow, both
artists being in part inspired by the
success of Turner's series *The Ports of
England*.

Between 1689 and 1851 the deep
anchorage of Falmouth Harbour,
protected by forts at Pendennis and
St Mawes, was the base for the Packet
Service that carried diplomatic mail
and bullion between England, the
Iberian Peninsula, the West Indies and
North and South America. The ships
shown in the background here are
probably the swift two- or three-masted
ten-gun brigs that carried these mails.

A View at Falmouth, Cornwall, about 1845,
watercolour with touches of bodycolour
over pencil by William Callow (1812–1908)

Overleaf: Hastings, East Sussex,
about 1843, watercolour and bodycolour
by John Martin (1789–1854)

Lancaster Sands, about 1826, watercolour by Joseph Mallord William Turner (1775–1851)

Overleaf: Littlehampton, West Sussex, 1919, watercolour and bodycolour with pen and black ink by Albert Goodwin (1845–1932)

July 1919

RURAL PEACE

THE WILD, remote scenery of North Wales attracted numerous artists at the end of the eighteenth century. John Varley made four tours in Wales between 1798 and 1802, gathering material that would serve as the basis for watercolours he subsequently exhibited at the Society of Painters in Water-Colours, of which he was a founder member in 1804. He was an important teacher who encouraged his pupils to sketch outdoors, although his own work came to rely on the somewhat schematized ideal compositions popularized in the three teaching manuals he published between 1815 and 1821. Here, however, in a simple but atmospheric study he is at his most direct and unaffected.

As well as the drama of its setting, Dolbadern Castle had potent historical associations for the late eighteenth century, a period preoccupied with defining notions of liberty. The Welsh prince Owain Goch had been imprisoned in Dolbadern by his brother Llewelyn from 1254 to 1277, when he was released by the Treaty of Conway that followed Edward I's defeat of independent Wales. In 1800, Turner chose this very subject for a major painting, exhibiting *Dolbadern Castle* with these lines:

> How aw[e]ful is the silence of the waste,
> Where nature lifts her mountains to the sky.
> Majestic solitude, behold the tower
> Where hopeless OWEN, long imprison'd, pined
> And wrung his hands for liberty, in vain.

Dolbadern Castle, Llanberis, about 1800,
watercolour by John Varley (1778–1842)

Between about 1826 and 1832 Palmer lived in seclusion as the leader of a group of young artists at Shoreham in the Darent Valley, Kent, which he described as his 'Valley of Vision'. His works of this period, with their immediately distinctive style, mark the apogee of his mystical celebration of nature, inspired by study of the Old Testament, Virgil and Milton. Here, in a picture that is itself a visionary experience, a shepherd makes his way through an exquisitely rendered depiction of a Kentish harvest landscape with his staff and dog. An enormous crescent moon, with Hesperus further off, bathes the scene in golden luminescence. In later years Palmer recalled the intense inspiration of his youth: 'Thoughts on RISING MOON, with raving-mad splendour of orange-twilight glow on landscape. I saw that at Shoreham'.

A Cornfield by Moonlight, with the Evening Star, about 1830, watercolour and bodycolour with pen and black ink, varnished, by Samuel Palmer (1805–81)

'THICK WOODS, green lanes and chequered shade' was how a contemporary critic summed up Redgrave's landscapes. To some extent, modest landscape studies of this sort were a private escape from a career increasingly devoted to arts administration, culminating in his appointment as Surveyor of the Royal Collection. In the 1850s he bought a cottage in Abinger, Surrey, where he made many drawings, watercolours and oil sketches from nature in the heavily wooded surroundings he particularly loved, and this example is characteristic.

A Stile, about 1860,
watercolour by
Richard Redgrave (1804–88)

Overleaf: Sunset in the Highlands,
about 1830, watercolour by
George Fennel Robson (1788–1833)

SCOTLAND and the poetry of Sir Walter Scott provided Robson with much of his inspiration. His first visit to the Highlands in 1810 was described by a fellow artist: 'That he might enter entirely into the romance of the country he dressed himself as a shepherd, and with Scott's poems in his pocket, he wandered over the mountains . . . fixing firmly in his mind the various aspects of nature, and collecting a fund of observations on which he might draw for the rest of his life'. Twilight scenes 'where he could dip his pencil in the purple gloom' were his favourite subjects.

WETHERBY, a market town on the River Wharfe north-east of Leeds, was a staging post on the Great North Road, where the London to Carlisle coach stopped. Girtin passed through in 1800, when he made a rapid pencil sketch on which he based this watercolour. The great arches of the ancient bridge form a dramatic motif, recalling Canaletto's unconventional views of the Thames through Westminster Bridge. Girtin further enhances the Italianate mood with the women at the water's edge, who seem like figures in a classical landscape.

Wetherby Bridge, Yorkshire
1800, watercolour over pencil
by Thomas Girtin (1775–1802)

Octr 8 10 - 1812

CLIFTON, an elegant Georgian suburb of Bristol, was regarded – like Bath – as a health resort. The novelist Fanny Burney, on a visit with her father in 1767, walked down the steep zig-zag path from Clifton Hill to the curative spring at Hotwells, where she set some scenes in *Evelina* (1778). In 1806, following the death of her father, Jane Austen and her mother lived briefly in Clifton, which later figured in several of her novels, notably *Northanger Abbey* (1818). A much-discussed proposed excursion to Clifton from Bath shocks Catherine Morland's uncle: 'Young men and women driving about the country in open carriages! Now and then it is very well, but going to inns and public places together! It is not right!' Some of the young people do go to Clifton, where they dine, visit the pump-room and eat ices at a pastry-cook's.

The River Avon at Clifton, 1813,
watercolour with pen and grey ink
by Thomas Stothard (1755–1834)

ELEN ALLINGHAM painted the cottages
and countryside of southern England to
record a rural way of life she feared would not
survive. By the 1880s, a period of agricultural
depression – together with the introduction of
mechanization in farming and the exodus of
labourers seeking employment in the expanding
cities – resulted in many ancient cottages falling
into ruin, being demolished or insensitively
modernized for new inhabitants: city commuters,
who were attracted by nostalgia for a supposedly
idyllic existence. In 1877, William Morris had
been influential in founding the Society for
the Protection of Ancient Buildings, one of
the earliest conservation groups, and Helen
Allingham shared many of his ideals. Her
watercolours, however, are far from being
strict architectural records; she was not above
prettifying her subjects in order to evoke the
character of the cottages and their inhabitants.

The cottage shown here still survives,
although its thatched roof has been replaced by
tiles and the surroundings have become less
rural.

Cowdray Cottage, Midhurst, Sussex, about 1890,
watercolour by Helen Allingham (1848–1926)

51

THE GREAT country house set in its estate had been a familiar subject in British art since the seventeenth century, emphasizing the social and political status of the owner. However, in this view made for an engraving, Paul Sandby has adopted a more subtle approach, showing us a bucolic landscape in which our attention is initially concentrated on the two foreground figures resting in the heat of the day, just like the hay-makers beyond them. Only then does the house become visible in the distance to the left. Hackwood Park was originally built for the 1st Duke of Bolton *c.* 1683–8, but between 1761 and 1763 the south front (visible here) was remodelled by John Vardy for the 5th Duke.

Hackwood Park, Hampshire, about 1775, watercolour with pen and grey ink by Paul Sandby (1730–1809)

John Dunstall fecit.

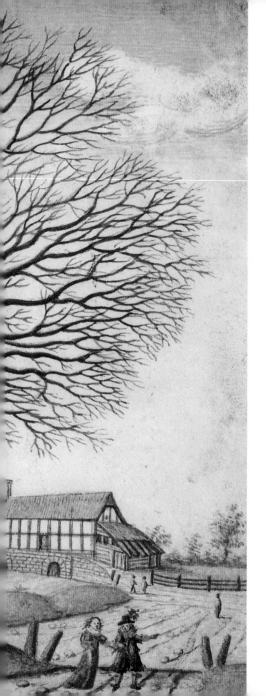

THE CHARM of this view of West Hampnett, a village near Chichester, West Sussex, lies in its appealing naivety. John Dunstall, a drawing master and etcher in the circle of Wenceslaus Hollar, seems to have been born locally, and he made a series of etchings of the neighbourhood. The foreground of this watercolour is dominated by an ancient pollard oak, whose mighty size is suggested by the diminutive figures. The red-brick gabled house, West Hampnett Place, was built in the late sixteenth century by Richard Sackville, and in the nineteenth century it served as a Workhouse. In the distance, beyond the mill, is a glimpse of Chichester Cathedral.

A Pollard Oak near West Hampnett Place, Chichester, about 1660, watercolour over black lead with touches of bodycolour on vellum by John Dunstall (d. 1693)

55

WORK AND INDUSTRY

J OSEPH WRIGHT, who was born and later worked in Derby, was one of the few eighteenth-century artists based outside London who made a significant contribution to the development of British painting, and the first major painter of subjects reflecting contemporary techno-logical innovations, which he was able to experience first-hand in the Midlands, the heart of the Industrial Revolution. Many of his patrons were closely involved with such developments, either as proprietors of industrial concerns or as scientists or inventors. Wright was attracted above all by the spectacle of these often highly dramatic processes, and intrigued by the effect they had on the participants and spectators.

Here Wright's subject is one of the most ancient industrial processes, the blacksmith at work, which gave him the opportunity to depict the dramatic lighting effects caused by the heat of the forge. The factual element is combined with a night-time setting, the figures illuminated to create a modern version of Vulcan's forge. The blacksmith's shop, with its glow of white-hot metal and din of hammering, was like a forecast of mighty changes to come, yet there is a human as well as an industrial element, with the seated figure gazing pensively into the distance and the two young boys standing near the anvil, one of whom has turned away from the heat while the other watches the smiths with rapt attention.

A Blacksmith's Shop, 1771,
mezzotint engraving by Richard Earlom (1743–1822)
after Joseph Wright of Derby (1734–97)

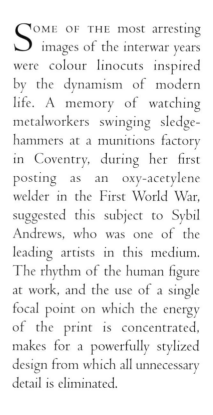

SOME OF THE most arresting images of the interwar years were colour linocuts inspired by the dynamism of modern life. A memory of watching metalworkers swinging sledge-hammers at a munitions factory in Coventry, during her first posting as an oxy-acetylene welder in the First World War, suggested this subject to Sybil Andrews, who was one of the leading artists in this medium. The rhythm of the human figure at work, and the use of a single focal point on which the energy of the print is concentrated, makes for a powerfully stylized design from which all unnecessary detail is eliminated.

Sledge-hammers, 1933, colour linocut by Sybil Andrews (1898–1992)

GÉRICAULT visited London in 1820 and again in 1821 to exhibit his famous painting *The Raft of the Medusa* and to make a series of lithographs. Most of these were equestrian subjects, while others were inspired by his observations of poverty in the streets of London. Contemporary events, often of a disturbing nature, were Géricault's chief preoccupation. Here his interest in everyday urban life inspired a watercolour of coalmen leading a laden coal wagon, which is being hauled by three powerful carthorses. Although not strictly topographically correct, St Paul's is shown in the distance, as if from the heights of north London, and an early steam-powered ship plies the Thames under a leaden sky.

The Coal Wagon, or Le Chariot, Route de Londres, about 1821, watercolour over black chalk by Théodore Géricault (1791–1824)

61

REAPERS.

Painted, Engraved & Published by Geo. Stubbs 1 Jan. 1791 N° 24 Somerset Street Portman Square London

Based on drawings he made while watching farm labourers at work, Stubbs's unsentimental yet sympathetic observation of rural life is here elevated by the heightened classical idiom of the composition, in which the figures are depicted in frieze-like poses as they cut and bind sheaves of corn or load a hay-cart. Both this and *Hay-Makers* (endpapers) are engravings after a pair of paintings exhibited by Stubbs at the Royal Academy in 1786 (now in Tate Britain). His contemporaries would probably have seen them as echoing passages in James Thomson's poem *The Seasons*, first published in 1726–30 and constantly reprinted throughout the eighteenth century.

Reapers, 1791, stipple engraving by George Stubbs (1724–1806)

THIS DRAWING is a leaf from a sketchbook Constable kept during June 1821, when he accompanied his friend and patron Archdeacon Fisher on a tour of the deaneries in Berkshire for which he was responsible, followed by a short visit to Oxford. The High, one of the city's main thoroughfares, has always impressed visitors with its handsome architecture, generous scale and graceful curve: in the previous year Wordsworth had written of 'the stream-like windings of that glorious street'. Constable's viewpoint here is between All Souls and The Queen's College, looking across to the seventeenth-century façade of University College, founded in 1249. Although architectural subjects are rare in Constable's work, this drawing with its subtle understanding both of structure and atmosphere shows him to be the equal of anyone.

The High Street, Oxford, 1821, pencil with grey wash by John Constable (1776–1837)

T HE RAILWAY LINES of the mid nineteenth century transformed
    the British urban landscape. Here, against a sunset sky, a train
makes its way through north London along a vast arched embankment
driven through a terrace of Georgian houses.

Railway Line at Camden Town, about 1860,
watercolour with touches of bodycolour
by Henry George Hine (1811–95)

Overleaf: View of a Manufacturing
Town, about 1870, watercolour
by Samuel Bough (1822–78)

THE ZENITH of British imperial power was reflected in the activity of the great ship-building yards of the Clyde and related heavy industry — between around 1880 and 1920, hundreds of thousands of men were employed in the yards that lined the banks of the river, the metal foundries and the coalmines of the region. Two-thirds of the nation's iron tonnage was launched into the Clyde, and Glasgow prided itself on being the second city of the empire. It was due to Scots innovation that wooden hulls were replaced by iron and steel, and Scots engineers developed and refined the steam engine. Many innovative vessels were built here, including the *Lusitania* in 1907, then the world's largest ship.

With the onset of the First World War, the Clyde shipyards were working at full stretch to supply the Admiralty. This wartime construction was recorded by the Glasgow-born Muirhead Bone, who was appointed in 1916 by the newly formed War Artists' Advisory Committee (WAAC) as Britain's first official war artist. He was initially posted to the Somme and then to the Clyde. In this drawing, a *tour de force* of observation taken from a very high viewpoint, we see a great ship taking shape on a slipway to the right, while tiny figures move around below us, dwarfed by the massive yet slender cranes. Bone's particular ability was in ordering a mass of visual detail into a powerful composition.

The Seven Cranes on the Clyde,
about 1917, pencil with brown wash
by Muirhead Bone (1876–1953)

D AZZLE CAMOUFLAGE for shipping was invented in 1917 during the First World War, inspired by pre-war abstract art. The intention was to confuse attackers as to the exact course a vessel was taking, by altering the perception of a ship's form through the use of strongly contrasting patterns of colour. The artist Edward Wadsworth was assigned to supervise the application of dazzle camouflage to Allied shipping in Bristol and Liverpool. After training at the Slade School of Art in London, he had been a signatory of the Vorticist manifesto published in *Blast* in 1914 and had shown work in the Vorticist exhibition in 1915 before serving as a naval intelligence officer in the Aegean. This is one of a series of woodcuts, made by Wadsworth immediately after the war, which were directly inspired by his camouflage work. He was also commissioned in 1919 by the Canadian War Memorials Fund to paint a large picture, *Dazzle-Ships in Drydock at Liverpool.*

The aesthetic qualities of dazzle painting captured the attention of the press, one writer describing it as 'suggestive of Futurism and Cubism', while another critic, writing about the 'Camouflage' exhibition held at the Royal Academy in 1919, remarked that 'the "dazzle" section illustrates amusingly an inversion of some of the principles of Post-Impressionism – how to destroy form instead of emphasising it – and the woodcuts of Mr Wadsworth are by far the best things artistically in the exhibition'.

Drydocked for Scaling and Painting, 1918,
woodcut by Edward Wadsworth (1889–1949)

Edward Wadsworth 1918.

THE WAR ARTISTS' Advisory Committee, initiated during the First World War, was revived shortly after the outbreak of the Second World War by Sir Kenneth Clark, then Director of the National Gallery. Henry Moore was among the artists commissioned to record the effects of the Blitz as well as to document the war effort on the Home Front. He had already begun to make a series of drawings inspired by the sight of people sheltering overnight in Underground stations during air raids. First and foremost a sculptor, Moore conceived his figures in terms of sculptural form, his motionless swathed subjects expressing a sense of timelessness. The fullest resolution of these studies came with his post-war monumental draped figure sculptures.

Moore, son of a mining engineer, was born in Castleford, Yorkshire and in December 1941 he was commissioned by WAAC to make drawings in Wheldale Colliery, where his father had worked. Just as the London Underground had intrigued him, so the claustrophobic subterranean world of the miners had a compelling quality that is evident from the annotated sketches he made on the spot, such as this sheet, using cheap tear-off pads of thin paper. Moore later said, 'I learned to use blackness as a base not white'. Yet, however spontaneous these studies were, they nevertheless have a frieze-like formality, recalling the classical sculpture Moore had drawn obsessively during visits to the British Museum when he was an art student in the 1920s.

Coalminers, 1942, pen and black ink
with black and yellow chalk and grey wash
by Henry Moore (1898–1986)

Positions   Miner sitting on his heels —   perhaps eating his snap
Picking — shovelling — picking up pieces of rock —   dry walling etc.

Born in St Ives in Cornwall, Lanyon studied locally and later at the Euston Road School in London. In the 1940s he was influenced by the constructivist work of Naum Gabo and Ben Nicholson, who had gone to live in St Ives in 1939. After the Second World War, when he served as an aero engineer, he returned to Cornwall and became increasingly attracted to American Abstract Expressionism. His feeling for his native surroundings emerged not in representational painting, but in compositions of abstracted shapes which are nevertheless extraordinarily expressive of the landscape.

Here his subject is an engine-house at East Pool, near Redruth, where tin had been mined for centuries. Production ceased in 1946, but the engine continued to pump out water until 1954, when a philanthropic American paid to preserve it. The Trevithick Trust and the National Trust have since opened this and another engine-house to the public. The last working tin mine in Cornwall, South Crofty, finally closed in 1998.

Old Mines at Pool, Cornwall, 1953,
black chalk and charcoal with touches of brown chalk
by Peter Lanyon (1918–64)

LEISURE

REACTING AGAINST the over-elaborate character of much Victorian graphic art, Nicholson introduced a bolder and simpler style, creating some of the most memorable visual images of the late nineteenth century. In 1898 he published *An Almanac of Twelve Sports*, choosing an appropriate pursuit to represent each month, including this woodcut of racing for March.

Racing, 1898, hand-coloured woodcut
by William Nicholson (1872–1949)

Overleaf: The Race for Doggett's Coat and
Badge, about 1800, watercolour with pen and
grey ink by Thomas Rowlandson (1756–1827)

THOMAS DOGGETT (d. 1721), a successful Irish-born comic actor and theatre manager in London, was a staunch Hanoverian who in 1715 instituted an annual rowing race between six young Thames Watermen (the taxi drivers of their day) to commemorate the anniversary of George I's accession to the throne, leaving instructions on his death that it was to be held 'for ever' – the prize was a silver badge and a distinctive coat. The contest still takes place today and is the oldest sculling race in the world. The original course was from the White Swan pub, London Bridge, to the Swan Inn at Chelsea, shown here on the right. In Rowlandson's characteristically lively watercolour, cheering spectators are urging on the oarsmen at the end of the race.

Trooping the Colour, Horseguards Parade, about 1800, watercolour with pen and brown and grey ink by Thomas Rowlandson (1756–1827)

ROWLANDSON shows a motley group of spectators observing this ceremony, which dates back to the early eighteenth century and since 1748 has also celebrated the Sovereign's birthday. The colours of the battalions are trooped down the ranks so that they may be seen and recognized by the troops.

THIS IS ONE of the earliest representa-
tions of golf, a game which Sandby
must have seen when he worked in
Scotland between 1747 and 1752. Golf had
been played informally since at least the
mid fifteenth century, the name probably
deriving from the old Scots verb 'to gowff',
meaning to cuff or strike hard, but not
until the mid eighteenth century were
clubs formed, and rules formulated. The
oldest clubs, the Honourable Company of
Edinburgh Golfers and the Edinburgh
Burgess Golfing Society, both originally
played over the five or six holes of the
Bruntsfield Links, shown here. In the foreground, a player in a scarlet coat, attended
by his caddy, is attempting to get out of a
bunker while behind him, another player
seems to be in pursuit of his ball. Beyond
is the distinctive silhouette of Edinburgh
Castle.

LE PRÉTEXTE

Se vend chez Martinet Rue du coq

Le Prétexte, 1815, hand-coloured etching
published by Aaron Martinet

WHILE TWO HIGHLANDERS inspect the produce offered for sale by a street vendor, two elegant ladies seated nearby have each found a pretext to peer under the soldiers' kilts in an attempt to satisfy their curiosity about what is worn (or not worn) beneath – one bends forward with a sideways glance, supposedly to tie the ribbon on her shoe, while the other pretends to play with the child.

Overleaf: The King's Bath and the Queen's Bath
at Bath, 1675, pen and black ink with grey wash
by Thomas Johnson (fl. *c.* 1628-1685)

'UP AT 4 A'CLOCK . . . called up to the *Bath* . . . by and by . . . came much company very fine ladies and the manner pretty enough only methinks it cannot be clean to go so many bodies together in to the same water . . . Strange to see what women and men herein that live all the season in these waters that cannot but be parboiled and look like the creatures of the Bath'.

Samuel Pepys, *Diary*, Saturday 13 June 1668

ueens bath
kithen in the two
is table on the wall
this thwortter
Dry Pume

Bladuds virthier
tho Boxton

amis Stonon of
tondor knight 1624

'WHO CAN DENY that bows and arrows are among the prettiest weapons in the world for feminine forms to play with? They prompt attitudes full of grace and power ... '. Thus George Eliot sets the scene for the fateful archery contest in *Daniel Deronda* (1876), at which Gwendolen Harleth meets her future husband, the selfish, arrogant and wealthy Grandcourt. Surprisingly, women were allowed to participate in the revival of archery towards the end of the eighteenth century – perhaps the first such sport before the introduction of croquet. Here a meeting of one of the early societies is shown.

A Meeting of the Society of British Archers in Gwersyllt Park, Denbighshire, 1794, watercolour with pen and brown ink over pencil by John Emes (fl. 1783–*c.* 1809) and Robert Smirke (1752–1845)

I N CONTRAST TO the perceived meagreness of continental cuisine, which was often disparaged as mere dressing-up of insubstantial ingredients, English food has always been characterized by its emphasis on meat. Hogarth's *O the Roast Beef of Old England* (1748) extolled meat as the symbol of British well-being and power.

This watercolour gives a rare glimpse of an early nineteenth-century middle-class supper table (the artist's own), including several kinds of cold meat, cheese and pies, accompanied by wine and perhaps beer – a simple though substantial supper. Mealtimes were changing rapidly: as Jane Austen records, in 1798 her family sat down to dinner at half past three, in 1805 they dine at four, occasionally at five; by 1808, 'we never dine now before five', while in fashionable households dinner was served at half past six. Supper too became later, in due course becoming a lighter alternative to dinner, and the widening gap between breakfast and dinner was filled by the introduction of luncheon. In *Pride and Prejudice* (1813), Jane Austen describes Lydia and Kitty Bennet buying salad and cucumber to add to cold meat, to make 'the nicest cold luncheon in the world'. In many working-class households dinner remained the main meal of the day, taken around noon, while tea, as a meal, was often a substitute for the dinner and supper of more prosperous families.

'Fragments on my own Supper Table', about 1805,
pencil and watercolour by John Hayward (1778–1822)

T HIS ANTHROPOMORPHIZED MAP shows Britain going to war with France in the form of King George III, his feet formed by Kent and Cornwall, his right arm and hand by Lancashire, Cheshire, Staffordshire and Warwickshire (holding, apparently, a joint of good British meat) and his tasselled nightcap by Northumberland, while two invented landmarks have been added near his face, 'Longhead Point' and 'Guzzle-guts Bay'. He craps vigorously, dispersing the French fleet in its course towards England. The 'British Declaration' emitting from John Bull's backside refers to a royal promise that the port of Toulon, then occupied by the British, would be restored to France on the restitution of its monarchy (which had been abolished the previous year, during the French Revolution).

Though the image is gross, the King's evacuations are heroic, patriotic and contemptuous, expressing the feelings of the brutish but uncensored John Bull, whom he here embodies.

'The French Invasion; – or – John Bull, bombarding the Bum Boats', 1793, hand-coloured etching by 'John Schoebert' (pseudonym for James Gillray, 1756–1815)

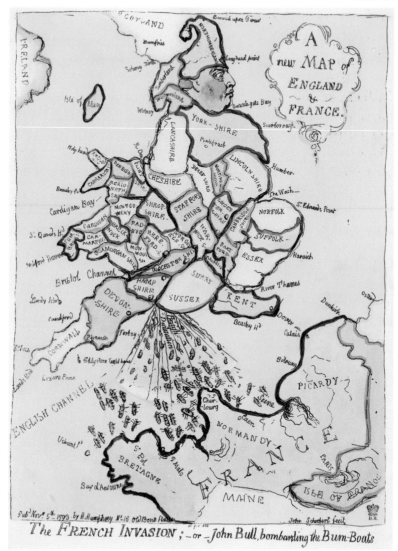

ILLUSTRATION REFERENCES

Photographs © The Trustees of the British Museum,
courtesy of the Department of Prints and Drawings